TELL ME
ABOUT
ARTISTS

VINCENT VAN GOGH

written by
John Malam

Evans

Evans Brothers Limited

Vincent van Gogh was an artist. He was born in Holland nearly 150 years ago. He painted most of his pictures in the last ten years of his short life. It was only after he died that people realised what a great artist he really was. This is his story.

Vincent painted this picture of himself when he was thirty-five years old.

Vincent van Gogh had three sisters and two brothers. Vincent was the eldest. His father, Theodorus, worked for the church as a preacher.

As a boy, Vincent liked to watch his mother, Anna, drawing. He began to make his own pictures. They were very good. He liked to read the Bible, too.

Holland is mostly flat, with many canals.

Vincent grew up in a village. People in the village said Vincent was rude and bad-tempered. The little boy with red hair and freckles hardly ever smiled. He always looked very serious.

Vincent when he was 13 years old

When Vincent was older, he often drew people working in the fields.

7

Vincent called his uncle 'Uncle Cent', which was short for Vincent.

Vincent's parents worried about him. He seemed to be unhappy. They said it was time for him to start work. So he went to work for his uncle. His uncle was an art dealer. He bought and sold paintings. Vincent liked his uncle and he enjoyed studying the paintings in his gallery.

Vincent worked in Paris in 1874.

Vincent learned about buying and selling paintings. To learn more, his uncle sent him to work in England and then in France.

When Vincent was twenty-three years old he left his job. He was unhappy again and had lost interest in paintings.

For a time he taught French at a school in Ramsgate, a town on the south coast of England.

The square in Ramsgate where Vincent lived in 1876

Then Vincent decided he wanted to work in the Church, like his father.

He went to Belgium to be a preacher. His first job was in a part of Belgium where there were many coal mines. He gave all his best clothes to the poor people he met. He wore ragged clothes and cared for the sick.

Vincent worked hard, but he soon discovered that he did not really want to be a preacher.

Vincent drew this picture in Belgium.

He remembered how he used to enjoy drawing and painting, and he began to wonder if he could become an artist.

Vincent had always got on well with his younger brother, Theo. Like Vincent, Theo had gone to work for their Uncle Cent, too. Theo had become an art dealer.

Theo, Vincent's brother

Vincent wrote to Theo and asked him for help. In his letter he said he felt trapped, like being in a "very dreadful cage".

Vincent wrote many letters to Theo. Theo often sent Vincent money to buy paints.

At first, all went well. Vincent studied famous artists of the past and began to make his first real drawings and paintings. He was very pleased with one of his paintings, called 'The Potato Eaters'.

Theo encouraged Vincent and for a time he was happy. But then, when he was about thirty years old, he began to think he had an illness. He thought he might be going mad.

When he was thirty-two, he moved to Paris to study painting. The other students made fun of him because he was a foreigner.

'The Potato Eaters'

▶ Vincent painted this picture of himself while he was in Paris.

13

After two years Vincent left Paris and went to Arles, a town in the south of France. He wanted to be near the sea, where the light was good and where he could paint different types of pictures. The year was 1888. Over the next twelve months he painted many of his most famous pictures.

Vincent painted this picture of his bedroom when he lived in Arles.

▼ Arles is on the River Rhône, not far from the Mediterranean Sea.

Vincent was a stranger in Arles. He had few friends. He asked the artist Paul Gauguin to visit him. But one night, the two men had an argument. Later that night, in a moment of madness, Vincent cut off his left ear lobe.

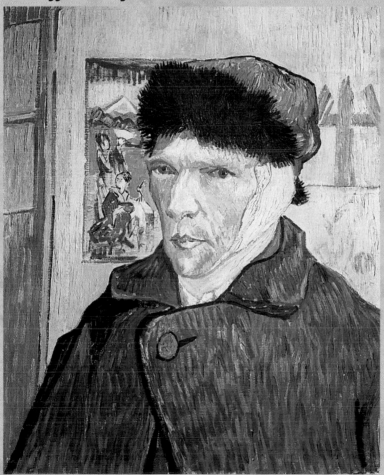

Vincent painted this picture of himself after he had cut off his ear lobe.

Vincent was a sick man. He had bad dreams. He went into hospital several times. He complained about the food and the other patients. The doctors could not help him, and so in the end he went home.

Even though he was still ill, Vincent continued to paint. He even painted when he was in hospital. His pictures were full of bright, swirling colours, painted with bold brushstrokes.

Vincent painted several pictures of this café in Arles.

He painted pictures of the countryside and its trees and flowers. He made pictures of the people he met and ordinary things such as chairs. He painted very quickly.

'Starry Night' has a big swirling sky.

In May, 1890, Vincent moved to the town of Auvers, near Paris.

One Sunday in July, just after lunch, he went for a walk in the countryside. He took his paints with him. Then something terrible happened. In another moment of madness, Vincent shot and wounded himself.

The doctors could not save him. His brother, Theo, was sent for. Two days after the shooting, Vincent died. He was thirty-seven years old.

'The Church at Auvers', one of Vincent's last paintings

▶ Vincent liked to paint pictures of ordinary things like his chair.

Vincent van Gogh died a poor man. In his own lifetime he only ever sold one painting. But almost one hundred years after his death, two of his pictures became the most expensive paintings in the world. In 1987, one sold for almost twenty-five million pounds and another for more than twenty-seven million pounds.

This painting of sunflowers is probably Vincent's most famous painting. It has become one of the world's most expensive pictures.

Important dates

1853 Vincent van Gogh was born in Holland

1857 Theo, Vincent's brother, was born

1869 Vincent began to work for his Uncle Cent, an art dealer

1873 He was sent to work in London, England

1874 He was sent to work in Paris, France

1876 He returned to England and taught at a school in Ramsgate

1877 He went to Amsterdam University in Holland to study religion

1878 He worked as a preacher in Belgium

1880 He decided to become an artist

1885 He painted 'The Potato Eaters'

1886 He moved to Paris, France

1888 He moved to Arles, France

1889 He went into hospital

1890 He moved to Auvers, France, where he died

Vincent's early drawings show the flat countryside of Holland where he was born.

Keywords

art dealer
someone who buys and sells drawings and paintings

artist
someone who makes drawings and paintings

gallery
a place where a dealer hangs pictures for people to see

preacher
a religious man who works for the Church and who speaks about God

Index

Anna, Vincent's mother 6
Arles 14, 15, 16
Auvers 18

Belgium 10
Bible, the 6

Church, the 10

England 9

France 9, 14

Gauguin, Paul 15

Holland 5, 6
hospital 16

Paris 8, 12, 13

Ramsgate 9

Theo, Vincent's brother 11, 13, 18
Theodorus, Vincent's father 6, 10

Uncle Cent 8, 11